Westin's
Trip to The
ZOO

Westin's Trip To The Zoo
is a fun filled book of Animals
and Rhymes. Going to the Zoo
is fun and exciting, adding some
rhymes makes it that much
more inviting. So come along and
have some fun. There's plenty
of room for everyone.

*Dedicated to my most
Favorite little Westin. Who
fills my heart with so much
love and joy. Such a
sweet and precious boy.
Growing so quick, by leaps
and bounds. Always turning
my frown upside down. I love
you so much, from now
till forever, your my sun-
shine, so bright so clever.
Much Love~GiGi*

THIS BOOK
BELONGS TO

Westin is going to the Zoo.
He thinks the animals are
very cool.
ZOO
WESTIN

First he see's a monkey in a tree. Swinging back and fort. Looks like fun to me.
WESTIN

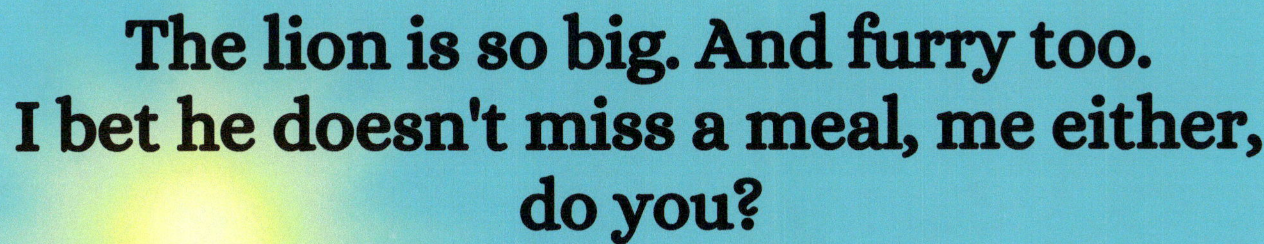

The lion is so big. And furry too.
I bet he doesn't miss a meal, me either,
do you?

Oh look! A mom and baby giraffe. Necks are so long. Could you imagine that?
WESTIN

Panda's are black
and white. And fun to see
They can climb so high,
up in a tree.
WESTIN

Walking around has made me so hungry. Time to fill my belly, yummy!

Alligators love the water. They swim very well. They have a green body and a long tail.

ZOO
WESTIN

Zebra's are like horses, but they have stripes. Making them different. And that is alright.
WESTIN

Elephant's are grey. Rhinoceroses are too. Both are very big, and eat a lot it's true.

Bears hibernate in the winter. They take a very long nap. When they wake up, they are ready for some trout.

North, South, East or
West, You won't get lost,
Use a map. It's the best.

Birds Snakes and Frogs too
are some of my favorites
found at the zoo.

I've had so much fun today at the zoo.

I can't wait until the next time, I go to the zoo. I hope you will come along with me. You too?

Bye For Now.